Margie

Double Trouble

Illustrated by
Yvonne Muller

Series Editor: Karen Morrison

About the Author

Margie Orford has spent most of her life in Namibia, and now lives in Windhoek with her family. She is very involved in issues relating to women and to the environment, working in both publishing and television as well as teaching.

Heinemann Educational Publishers
Halley Court, Jordan Hill, Oxford OX2 8EJ
A division of Reed Educational & Professional Publishing Ltd

Heinemann Educational Books (Nigeria) Ltd
PMB 5205, Ibadan
Heinemann Educational Botswana Publishers (Pty) Ltd
PO Box 10103, Village Post Office, Gaborone, Botswana

FLORENCE PRAGUE MADRID ATHENS
MELBOURNE AUCKLAND TOKYO SINGAPORE KUALA LUMPUR
PORTSMOUTH NH (USA) MEXICO CITY CHICAGO
SAO PAULO JOHANNESBURG KAMPALA NAIROBI

© Margie Orford 1996
First published by Heinemann Educational Publishers in 1996
The right of Margie Orford to be identified as the author of this work has been asserted by her in accordance with the Copyright, Designs and Patents Act 1988

British Library Cataloguing in Publication Data
A catalogue record for this book is available
from the British Library

ISBN 0 435 89184 7

Glossary
Difficult words are listed alphabetically on page 29

Edited by Christine King
Designed by The Point
Printed and bound by George Over Ltd, Rugby and London

96 97 98 99 10 9 8 7 6 5 4 3 2 1

Honey and Mersia were waiting for their father. He was coming to take them home for the school holidays. They lived on Bitter Water Farm, where their father was the manager.

After a while Honey shouted, 'There's Dad, Mersia!'

They both smiled as they watched the donkey cart bumping along the dusty road. As soon as Joseph, their father, stopped, the twins ran to hug him.

Joseph hugged them both. 'Hello, Honey. Hello, Mersia,' he said. 'Now which one is which?'

They all laughed. The twins were identical – short hair, long thin legs and sparkling eyes. Only their mother could tell them apart. She called them 'Double Trouble'.

The twins threw their bags into the cart and climbed up next to their father.

As they rode along, the girls made plans for the long December holidays. Their father didn't join in. He was very quiet.

Gradually, Honey and Mersia realised that their father was worried about something. The twins didn't need to talk to each other to know what the other was thinking. All they needed was their 'special look'.

When they stopped for lunch, the twins asked together, 'What's wrong, Dad?'

Joseph sighed. 'There's no point hiding it from you,' he said. 'I'm very worried. There are poachers in the area. They've killed animals on all the farms near us. And they're violent. They beat old Simon very badly.

'We are lucky. There has been no poaching on Bitter Water yet. But your mother and I think it will come.'

This news upset Honey and Mersia and they were quiet for the rest of the journey.

As they rode up the farm road, the twins grew excited again. But something was very wrong at home! Two police trucks were parked near the house. Several policemen were standing about. The twins recognised Captain Nyambe. He was standing next to their mother, who was crying and shaking her head.

As the cart stopped, Captain Nyambe and the other policemen walked towards it. They did not look at all friendly.

'Where were you last night, Joseph?' asked Captain Nyambe.

'I was on the road into town to fetch the twins,' replied Joseph sharply. 'Here they are, back home for the school holidays. What is this all about? Why is Magdalena crying?'

The twins knew their father was getting angry.

'You'd better watch out, Joseph,' warned Captain Nyambe. 'The gun used to shoot those two kudu is the same as yours.'

He pointed to the two dead animals in the back of his truck. The twins noticed them for the first time. They both shivered.

'You know that I would never poach, Nyambe!' shouted Joseph. 'Now get out of here or there'll be trouble!'

The police climbed into their trucks.

'We'll be watching your every move, Joseph,' warned Captain Nyambe.

'Yes, soon you'll be in prison,' another policeman taunted him.

The trucks pulled away in a cloud of dust.

Joseph put his arms around Magdalena. The twins hugged their mother too. 'Don't worry, Mum,' they whispered.

Honey and Mersia gave each other their special look. They were going to find out the truth. No one could call their father a poacher and get away with it.

Next morning, another unwelcome visitor arrived. He was Paul Beukes, a cruel and bitter man. He worked for Joseph, but he hated doing it. He had always been jealous of Joseph's job as manager.

He had always tried to hurt Honey and Mersia. He used to hit or kick them when their mother wasn't looking. When they were smaller he had really hurt them at times. But now they were twelve years old, they were much too quick for him.

The twins hated Paul Beukes.

'I am going to become farm manager when your father goes to jail,' said Paul.

He smiled nastily at the girls and kicked Mersia's leg. Honey was too quick for him. But she gave her sister a special look. Yes, Mersia had seen them too! There were bloodstains on Paul Beukes' shoes.

Honey and Mersia decided without talking that they were going to follow Paul. They felt he had something to do with the poachers.

Honey and Mersia watched Paul all afternoon. He left the farm as it began to get dark. Only the twins noticed him sneaking off. No one else took any notice because they were all busy.

The twins followed him at a safe distance. He was carrying something but it was too dark to see what it was.

The night grew darker and darker. An owl hooted and the twins jumped with fear. They held each other's hand and gave each other a special look. This look said, 'Let's be brave and help save Dad's good name.'

They followed Paul silently, hand in hand. After a long walk they reached a crossroads. Paul stopped and sat down on the side of the road.

The twins crouched down behind a dead tree and watched carefully. Suddenly they heard the noise of a car. It was coming towards them without lights on.

The car stopped and a man got out. Mersia and Honey looked at each other. It was the policeman who had taunted their father. Paul stood up, and both men laughed quietly. The twins had to listen hard to hear what they were saying.

'I can't wait to see Joseph's face when you arrest him,' Paul said.

'Have you got his gun?' asked the policeman. 'We're going to need it when we shoot those two white rhinos tonight. Everyone will think Joseph shot them! I can get Nyambe to arrest him tomorrow. We'll sell the horns in Windhoek and no one will ever suspect us. We'll be rich!'

The men laughed again and arranged to meet back at the crossroads at midnight.

As the men went their separate ways, Mersia whispered, 'What shall we do?'

'Let's fetch Captain Nyambe. We haven't got time to go home,' said Honey.

The police station was quite near. The twins walked quickly through the bush. They were afraid to walk along the road in case Paul or the policeman saw them.

Captain Nyambe was about to go to bed when they arrived, but he let them in. They quickly told him what they had seen.

'I don't believe you,' said Captain Nyambe angrily. 'That man is my personal assistant.'

'Please, please, Captain Nyambe,' begged the twins. 'It's true. Please believe us. We're not lying to you.'

'Well!' declared Captain Nyambe. 'You two are known as Double Trouble with all your tricks! If you are making this up you will be in Double Trouble with me!'

The twins said nothing, but they gave each other their special look.

Captain Nyambe followed them into the dark night. When they reached the crossroads all three of them hid behind the dead tree. They waited silently until it was nearly midnight.

Honey looked at Mersia just as Paul appeared. He was carrying Joseph's gun! A few minutes later they heard a low whistle and the policeman appeared. He was holding a machine-gun. Honey and Mersia began to feel really scared.

The two poachers walked through the veld. Captain Nyambe and the twins followed them. Soon they reached a high game fence. The two rare white rhinos lived in safety on the other side of the fence.

Paul and the policeman quickly cut a hole in the fence, and slipped through silently. Captain Nyambe waited for a short time. Then he too climbed through the hole in the fence. The twins were about to follow but he stopped them.

'It's too dangerous for you,' Captain Nyambe said. 'I have no gun. Go home and fetch Joseph and other men to help.'

He turned and disappeared into the darkness.

The twins gave each other a look. They didn't have to say anything! It was a long way to their house. To save the rhinos they would need to get help quickly.

The nearest house belonged to the farmer who owned the game farm. But that was on the other side of the fence.

Without saying a word, Honey and Mersia climbed through the hole and ran through the dark bush. Soon they reached the farm house. There were no lights on, but they banged on the door and woke the farmer, Mr Smit.

'Come quickly! Get help! Poachers!' said Mersia.

'Bring your gun, Mr Smit. They want to kill your rhinos!' said Honey.

Mr Smit grabbed his gun and ran to wake his game guards.

The men were very worried. They told the twins that the female rhino had a new calf.

'Oh no!' said the twins together. They knew that if the poachers killed the mother, the baby would also die.

'We know where the rhinos are – we saw them earlier,' said Jan, one of the game guards. 'We'll go and wait there. Don't you worry. You two girls are Double Trouble for those poachers!'

Jan led the way into the bush. The other men walked quickly and quietly after him, followed by the twins.

After a while they climbed up a little koppie and looked down. There stood the rhinos. They looked like grey ghosts in the darkness.

'We'll hide here,' whispered Jan. 'The wind is blowing this way, so the animals won't smell us. This is the way the poachers will have to come. Don't make a sound.'

They waited for a while. Then the twins heard a faint noise. Honey touched Jan's arm and pointed behind them. There were Paul and the policeman.

The poachers walked past the waiting group and lay down on the ground. Then they pointed their guns at the rhinos.

Mr Smit and his game guards stepped out of the shadows.

'Drop your guns and put your hands up!' said Jan. He sounded very angry.

'You are both under arrest,' said a loud voice.

It was Captain Nyambe. Honey and Mersia had forgotten all about him. They both gave him a big hug.

Paul Beukes saw the twins. 'Not them!' he spat. 'Double Trouble!'

The twins gave each other their special look. Paul glared at them as Captain Nyambe took him and his evil friend off to jail.

Mr Smit and the game guards were very grateful. Mr Smit fetched his truck and drove Honey and Mersia home.

Joseph and Magdalena had been sick with worry. They both rushed out as soon as they heard the truck.

'Where have you been? We've been so worried,' said Joseph and Magdalena, hugging their daughters.

'You have two brave daughters,' said Mr Smit. 'Very brave and very clever. Here is something to help them with their education.'

He handed Magdalena an envelope full of money. Then he told Magdalena and Joseph the whole story.

'I am very proud of you both,' said Joseph.

'And I am very happy that my husband won't be going to jail,' said Magdalena.

The twins just smiled. They were really tired.

Mr Smit looked at the twins and said, 'Hey, I could use some Double Trouble on my farm. Would you girls like a holiday job?'

'Yes please!' the twins shouted together.

'Come and see me tomorrow. Jan needs some help with the rhinos,' said Mr Smit, getting back into his truck.

The twins looked at each other. But they didn't need their special look to know what the other was thinking. It was going to be a great holiday!

Questions

1 Why were Honey and Mersia waiting for their father?

2 Why do you think people called Honey and Mersia 'Double Trouble'?

3 How did the twins tell each other things without talking?

4 What were the police doing at the twins' home?

5 What did Paul Beukes do to make the twins hate him?

6 How did the twins find the poachers?

7 Where did the twins go to fetch help to stop the poachers?

8 When did Mr Smit and the game guards stop the poachers?

9 What reward did Honey and Mersia get for saving the rhinos?

Activities

1 Mr Smit says that the twins are brave and clever. Write down some other words which you think describe the twins.

2 Rhinos are endangered animals. There are not many of them left in the world, so they are protected by law. Find out which animals are endangered in your country.

3 Choose one endangered animal. Draw a picture of it in your book. Discuss why this animal has become endangered.

Glossary

crossroads (page 12) place where two roads meet
crouched (page 13) bent down very low
glared (page 24) stared angrily
identical (page 2) exactly the same
koppie (page 22) the Afrikaans word for a small hill
poachers (page 4) people who kill animals which are protected by law, or which belong to someone else
sneaking (page 11) moving carefully and quietly so as not to be seen
suspect (page 14) believe that someone is guilty of a crime
taunted (page 8) mocked in a nasty way

The Junior African Writers Series is designed to provide interesting and varied African stories both for pleasure and for study. There are five graded levels in the series.

Level 2 is for readers who have been studying English for four to five years. The content and language have been carefully controlled to increase fluency in reading.

Content The plots are simple and the number of characters is kept to a minimum. The information is presented in small manageable amounts and the illustrations reinforce the text.

Language Reading is a learning experience and, although the choice of words is carefully controlled, new words, important to the story, are also introduced. These are contextualised and explained in the glossary.

Glossary Difficult words which learners may not know have been listed alphabetically at the end of the book. The definitions refer to the way the word is used in the story, and the page reference is for the word's first use.

Questions and **Activities** The questions give useful comprehension practice and ensure that the reader has followed and understood the story. The activities develop themes and ideas introduced, and can be done as pairwork or groupwork in class, or as homework.

JAWS Starters
In addition to the five levels of JAWS titles, there are three levels of JAWS Starters. These are full-colour picture books designed to lead in to the first level of JAWS.